THE CROSSROADS OF SHOULD AND MUST

FIND AND FOLLOW YOUR PASSION

ELLE LUNA

WORKMAN PUBLISHING · NEW YORK

Copyright © 2015 by Elle Luna

Illustrations copyright © 2015 by Elle Luna

Library of Congress Cataloging-in-Publication Data is available.

ISBN 978-0-7611-8488-1

Book design by Elle Luna

Workman books are available at special discounts when purchased in bulk for premiums and sales promotions as well as for fund-raising or educational use. Special editions or book excerpts can also be created to specification. For details, contact the Special Sales Director at the address below, or send an email to specialmarkets@workman.com.

Workman Publishing Co., Inc.
225 Varick Street
New York, NY 10014-4381
workman.com

WORKMAN is a registered trademark of Workman Publishing Co., Inc.

Printed in China

First printing March 2015

10 9 8 7 6 5 4

FOR MY FAMILY

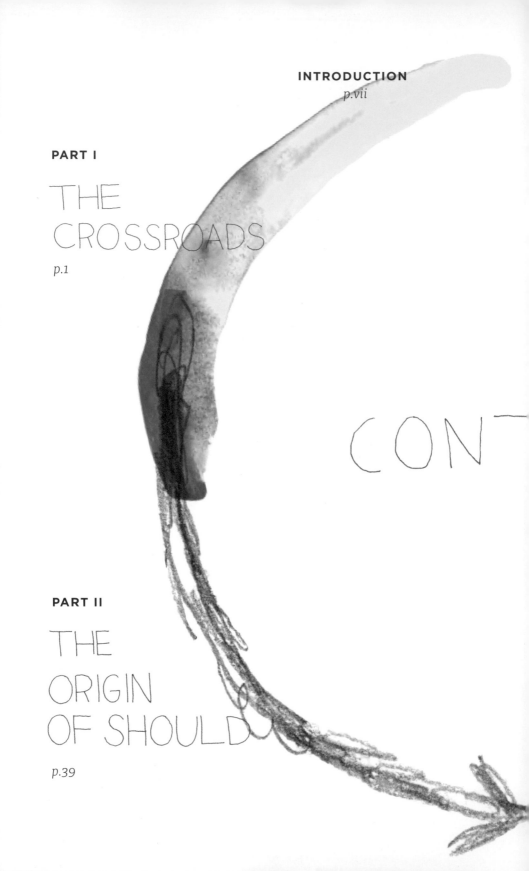

Publish

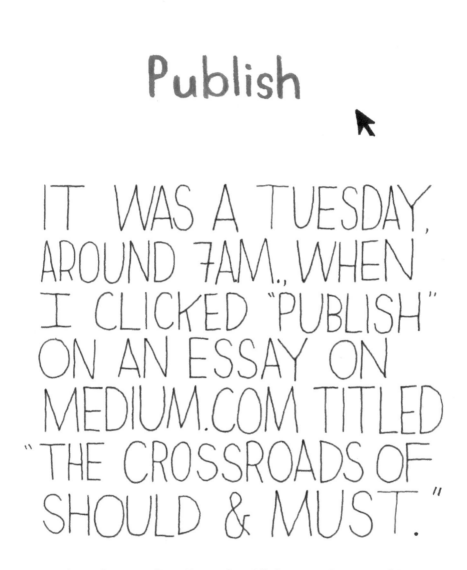

IT WAS A TUESDAY, AROUND 7 A.M., WHEN I CLICKED "PUBLISH" ON AN ESSAY ON MEDIUM.COM TITLED "THE CROSSROADS OF SHOULD & MUST."

We share things online. Every day. All the time. But something about *this* thing was different. So different, that in a few short weeks, it was tweeted to over five million people and read by over a quarter million readers.

"Drop everything you're doing and read this right now," one woman posted. "This article changed my life," wrote another. "I was about to send it to all of my employees," wrote one CEO, "but I assumed that a third of them would quit if they read it. But you know what? If they don't want to be here, I want them to quit—so I sent it."

The emails poured in. The tweets lit up my phone. The article spread through the Web in a flash, and then flashed some more. It continued to shine and grow and, well, here we are. I decided to write this book because of the people who shared their stories with me and the pain and courage I felt in their struggle. Women in their thirties. Men in their twenties. A high school senior. Fathers. A widow. Single moms. Millionaires who were poor. Poor people who were millionaires. Teachers. Lawyers. A musician disguised as a lawyer. A poet who loved to drive a city bus. Women who didn't want kids. Fathers who wanted to raise kids. People who felt stuck in their jobs and people who were so desperately grateful to have a job at all.

The pain cut across gender, location, and age. And at its essence, the pain was this—

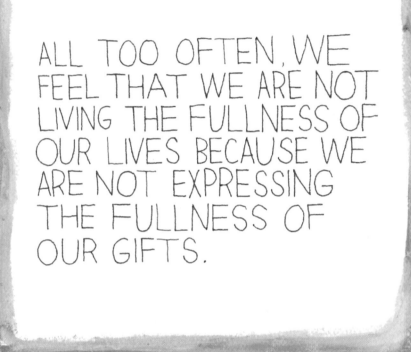

ALL TOO OFTEN, WE FEEL THAT WE ARE NOT LIVING THE FULLNESS OF OUR LIVES BECAUSE WE ARE NOT EXPRESSING THE FULLNESS OF OUR GIFTS.

I heard from people who seemed willing to do anything to make their dissatisfaction go away, but they didn't know what to do.

I wrote this book to share what I have found most helpful in navigating my own journey, as well as what has been most helpful for the people I met. However, you're not holding a book of answers, because only you know those; you're holding a collection of the most effective questions I encountered along the way. Think of these pages as a series of doorways designed so that you can choose which way your journey will go.

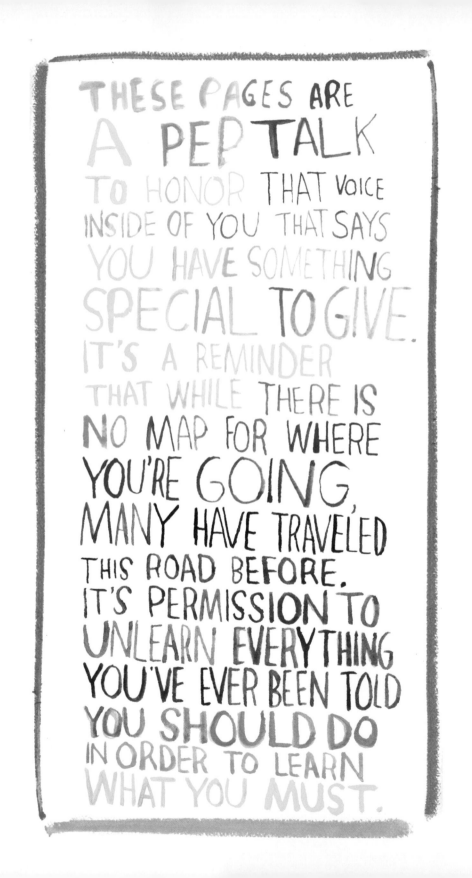

THESE PAGES ARE A PEP TALK TO HONOR THAT VOICE INSIDE OF YOU THAT SAYS YOU HAVE SOMETHING SPECIAL TO GIVE. IT'S A REMINDER THAT WHILE THERE IS NO MAP FOR WHERE YOU'RE GOING, MANY HAVE TRAVELED THIS ROAD BEFORE. IT'S PERMISSION TO UNLEARN EVERYTHING YOU'VE EVER BEEN TOLD YOU SHOULD DO IN ORDER TO LEARN WHAT YOU MUST.

It's 11:55 a.m. on a Thursday, and I'm clicking "Save" on this document one final time before it begins its adventure into the world. In my own life, I've found that things appear at the ideal time. Not before. And not after. Consider the possibility that this book made its way into your hands because you wanted it to. Because a part of you has seen a crossroads in your life, and you're ready for the journey ahead. I am humbled and grateful that these words will find their way from me to you, somehow, in some way, at just the right time. Thank you for being a part of this wild and wondrous journey. From one fellow traveler to another—*Godspeed*.

October 23, 2014
San Francisco, CA

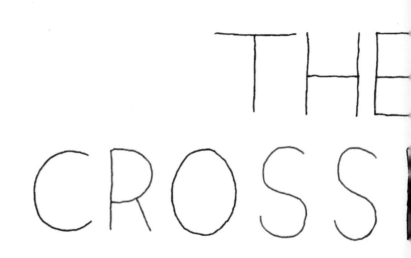

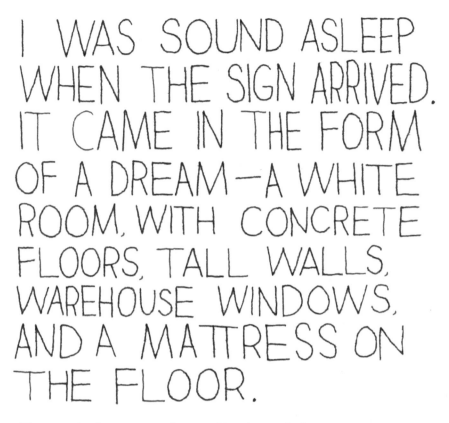

I WAS SOUND ASLEEP WHEN THE SIGN ARRIVED. IT CAME IN THE FORM OF A DREAM—A WHITE ROOM, WITH CONCRETE FLOORS, TALL WALLS, WAREHOUSE WINDOWS, AND A MATTRESS ON THE FLOOR.

That was it; that was my dream. Simple, easily forgotten, yet recurring—nightly—for months. One day, a friend asked the question that turned my life inside out. She said, *"Have you ever tried to look for your dream in real life?"* Her question felt like a drawbridge being lowered, an invitation to step into a world that felt equal parts fascinating and ridiculous. I first refused to consider it, but her question lingered, and eventually, I began to wonder . . .

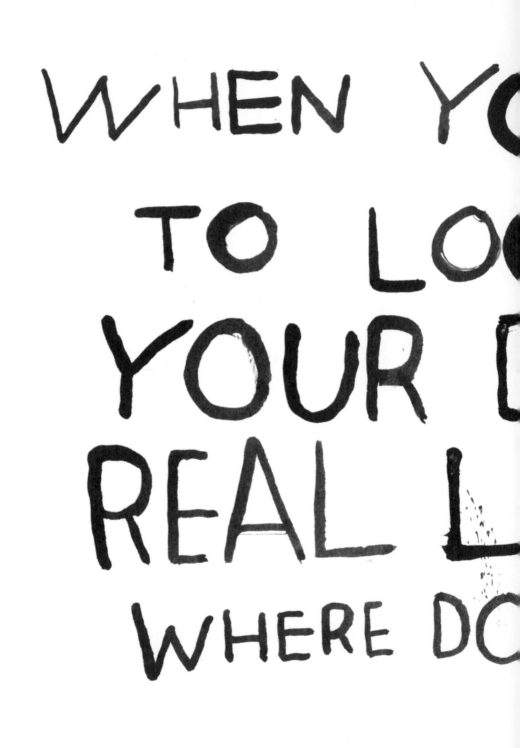

U DECIDE

K FOR

REAMS IN

FE,

YOU GO?

CRAIGSLIST, I THOUGHT.

white room from dreams?|

I felt silly scanning the website's apartment rental listings. What would I even type in the search box? I had no idea what I was looking for or what I would find. But the quest became this alluring, playful adventure, like being on a treasure hunt.

And one day, I found it. Right there on the website in a small photograph not much bigger than a thumbnail. The white room—there it was, right there, on the computer screen. An apartment for rent in San Francisco. And there was an open house the very next day—*of course*.

BILL MOYERS:

DO YOU EVER HAVE THE SENSE
OF... BEING HELPED BY HIDDEN HANDS?

JOSEPH CAMPBELL:

ALL THE TIME. IT IS MIRACULOUS.
I EVEN HAVE A SUPERSTITION THAT
HAS GROWN ON ME AS A RESULT OF
INVISIBLE HANDS COMING ALL THE TIME—
NAMELY, THAT IF YOU DO FOLLOW
YOUR BLISS YOU PUT YOURSELF ON
A KIND OF TRACK THAT HAS BEEN
THERE ALL THE WHILE, WAITING FOR
YOU. AND THE LIFE THAT YOU OUGHT
TO BE LIVING IS THE ONE YOU ARE
LIVING. WHEN YOU CAN SEE THAT,
YOU BEGIN TO MEET PEOPLE WHO
ARE IN YOUR FIELD OF BLISS, AND
THEY OPEN DOORS TO YOU. I SAY,
FOLLOW YOUR BLISS AND DON'T
BE AFRAID, AND DOORS WILL OPEN
WHERE YOU DIDN'T KNOW THEY
WERE GOING TO BE.

JOSEPH CAMPBELL
THE POWER OF MYTH

When I arrived at the open house, I was surprised to find a dozen other people viewing the apartment. That was not a part of my dream. But in some inexplicable way, I felt that the space was already mine, that it *had* to be, that just as I was searching for it, it was searching for me, and while I had no idea what I was doing, I knew exactly what I was doing. I gave the agent my rental application and left.

Two weeks later, with two suitcases and the dog, I moved into the white room from my dreams. I sat on the concrete floor and looked around. Unexpectedly, I began to panic. What had I done? What was this all about?

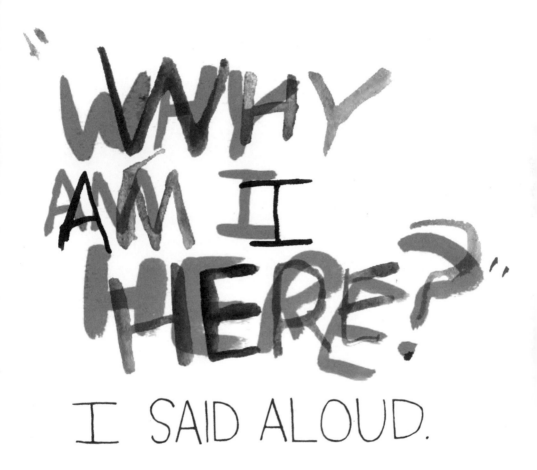

"WHY AM I HERE?"

I SAID ALOUD.

And the room replied—"It's time to paint."

The next morning, I began the hardest journey of my life—painting my dream.

I hadn't painted in almost ten years, so I went to the art supply store and rebuilt my tool kit.

FOAM BRUSHES & FOAM ROLLERS & FAN BRUSHES AND INK

As I ran my hands over the wooden brush handles, I recalled my brush-in-hand childhood, that magic wand that transformed forest sticks into brightly colored snakes, rocks into round canvases, paper plates into portraits. I collected memories into the cart as the familiar smell of fibrous papers lured me to the next aisle.

KRAFT & WATERCOLOR AND COLD-PRESSED COTTON PAPERS

I grabbed what I needed and made my way into the colors.

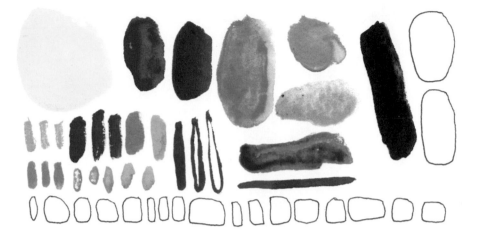

How quickly I remembered their names, their consistencies, their subtle shifts when mixed with water or gloss, their reactions to Mylar and Bristol and unprimed canvas. I remembered being eighteen years old and leaving my childhood home, gathering my favorite pencils and paints and placing them in that box that we sealed with thick, gummy tape. I placed the box into the trunk of the car, waved good-bye, and reversed out of the driveway, heading north.

At the art supply store, as I heaved a gallon tub of white paint off the shelf and into my cart, I remembered the weight of a similar box in my hands as I carried it up the stairs to my first apartment. My second. The ninth and tenth. I kept that box next to desks where it remained unopened, I forced it into cabinets so that it wouldn't be in the way, and eventually, while I was filling out law school applications, I abandoned it in the basement of an old apartment building next to a faux Christmas tree with pre-strung lights.

Stepping into my future, I paid for my art supplies, returned home with my box, and painted with an energy that I'd never felt before.

THE ONLY CATCH?

I had a full-time job, working over forty hours a week on a startup that I cared about deeply. I was a part of a small group of people who wanted to change how people interacted with their email. We were working quietly, intensely, for the better part of a year, taking an idea on a Post-it Note all the way through to an implemented product in Apple's App Store. When I wasn't designing, I was painting. I felt that I had entered one of the most creative periods of my life. But it was neither balanced nor sustainable, and I sensed that I was quickly approaching a crossroads in my life.

I was talking about all of this to a friend when he asked, "Have you seen that TED talk by Stefan Sagmeister?" Scooping up his laptop and sitting next to me, he said, "We must watch it right now."

In the talk, Sagmeister, an artist and designer working in New York City, defines the difference between jobs, careers, and callings. I had never thought about them as different things.

A JOB

Something typically done from 9 to 5 for pay.

A CAREER

A system of advancements and promotions over time where rewards are used to optimize behavior.

A CALLING

Something that we feel compelled to do regardless of fame or fortune; the work is the reward.

THE COOLEST BUSINESS
CARD OF ALL TIME

I began to wonder which ones I had in my life. And I ask you the same question—

WHICH OF THESE DO YOU CURRENTLY HAVE— A JOB? A CAREER? OR A CALLING?

Another manifestation of this appeared while I was reading Arianna Huffington's biography of Pablo Picasso.

In it, she describes how Picasso balanced work and life, saying:

> The more I discovered about his life and the more I delved into his art, the more the two converged. "It's not what an artist does that counts, but what he is," Picasso said. But his art was so thoroughly autobiographical that what he did was what he was.

PICASSO'S LIFE

PICASSO'S ART

PICASSO'S LIFE

PICASSO'S ART

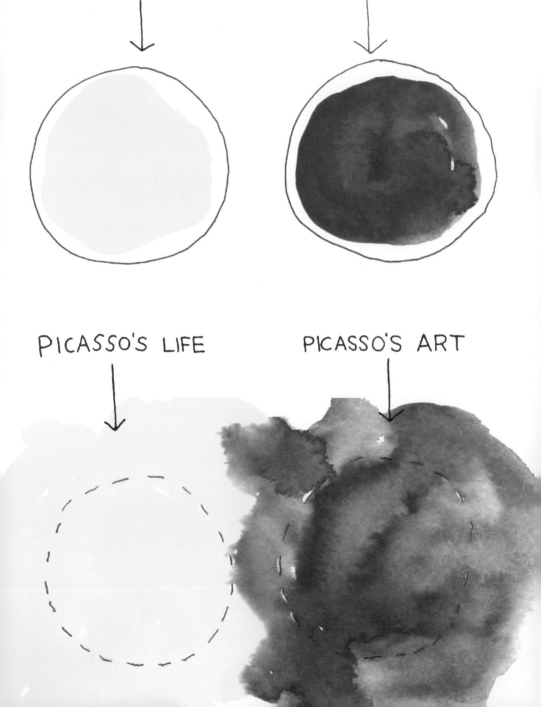

Yes, Picasso had incredible talent, but the secret to his genius was this—Picasso's life blended seamlessly with his work.

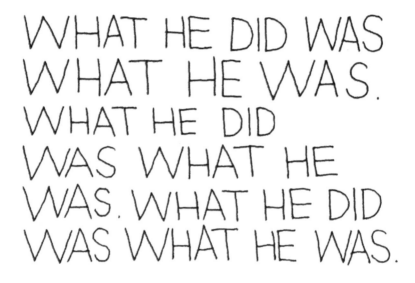

WHAT HE DID WAS WHAT HE WAS. WHAT HE DID WAS WHAT HE WAS. WHAT HE DID WAS WHAT HE WAS.

I could not stop reading that sentence. It felt like the key that unlocked a thousand doors. It was impossible to tell where his life ended and his paintings began. It was all one huge swirling mix of bullfights and beaches and brushes.

This led me to a hypothesis. What if . . .

OUR

JOB

=

OUR

CAREER

=

OUR

CALLING

What if who we are and what we do become one and the same? What if our work is so thoroughly autobiographical that we can't parse the product from the person? In this place, job descriptions and titles no longer make sense; we no longer *go* to work, we *are* the work.

WHO YOU ARE

↓

WHAT YOU DO

Back at the startup, it was 9 a.m. on Thursday, February 7, when we shared our app with the world. The launch was an unmitigated success, and I knew that this moment was one of the highlights of my life. In the back of my mind, I couldn't help wondering what any of it had to do with my dream of a white room.

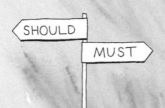

I WAS SITTING AT MY DESK
WHEN THE CROSSROADS
APPEARED. THE CHOICE WAS
CLEAR. TWO WORLDS—
EQUALLY APPEALING.
BUT THEY WERE DIFFERENT.
I LOOKED AT MY FINANCES,
SAW THAT I COULD BUY
MYSELF A FEW MONTHS
TO TRY TO MAKE A LIVING
AS AN ARTIST, AND I PUT
IN MY TWO WEEKS' NOTICE.
I HAD NO IDEA WHAT I WAS
DOING; I KNEW EXACTLY
WHAT I WAS DOING.

"LET YOU
SILENTLY
BY THE STR
OF WHA
LOV
IT WILL NOT

RSELF BE

DRAWN

NGE PULL

T YOU REALLY

E.

EAD YOU ASTRAY."

RUMI
POET

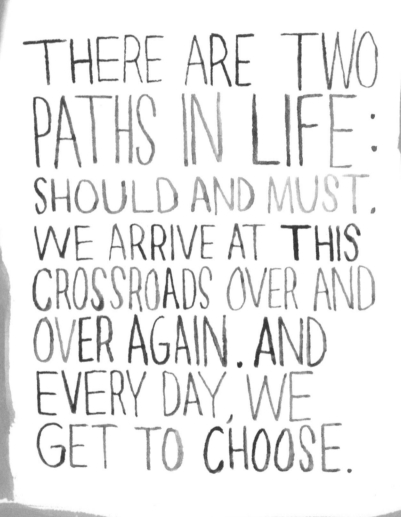

THERE ARE TWO PATHS IN LIFE: SHOULD AND MUST. WE ARRIVE AT **THIS** CROSSROADS OVER AND OVER AGAIN. AND EVERY DAY, WE GET TO CHOOSE.

Should is how other people want us to live our lives.

It's all of the expectations that others layer upon us. Sometimes, Shoulds are small, seemingly innocuous, and easily accommodated. "You should listen to that song," for example. At other times, Shoulds are highly influential systems of thought that pressure and, at their most destructive, coerce us to live our lives differently.

When we choose Should, we're choosing to live our life for someone or something other than ourselves. The journey to Should can be smooth, the rewards can seem clear, and the options are often plentiful.

Must is different.

Must is who we are, what we believe, and what we do when we are alone with our truest, most authentic self. It's that which calls to us most deeply. It's our convictions, our passions, our deepest held urges and desires—unavoidable, undeniable, and inexplicable. Unlike Should, Must doesn't accept compromises.

Must is when we stop conforming to other people's ideals and start connecting to our own—and this allows us to cultivate our full potential as individuals. To choose Must is to say yes to hard work and constant effort, to say yes to a journey without a road map or guarantees, and in so doing, to say yes to what Joseph Campbell called "the experience of being alive, so that our life experiences on the purely physical plane will have resonance within our innermost being and reality, so that we actually feel the rapture of being alive."

Choosing Must is the greatest thing we can do with our lives.

Vincent van Gogh chose Must when he continued to paint, canvas after canvas, even as the world rejected his art. His work went largely unrecognized while he was alive. It can be challenging to understand, in our hyperconnected world of likes and comments and follows, what being truly, utterly unseen might have felt like. In a letter to his brother Theo in 1882, he describes such a feeling—

"WHAT AM I IN THE EYES OF
MOST PEOPLE—A NONENTITY,
AN ECCENTRIC, OR AN
UNPLEASANT PERSON—
SOMEBODY WHO HAS NO
POSITION IN SOCIETY AND
WILL NEVER HAVE; IN SHORT,
THE LOWEST OF THE LOW.
ALL RIGHT, THEN—EVEN IF
THAT WERE ABSOLUTELY
TRUE, THEN I SHOULD LIKE
TO SHOW BY MY WORK
WHAT SUCH AN ECCENTRIC,
SUCH A NOBODY, HAS IN
HIS HEART."

VINCENT VAN GOGH

A lawyer in his thirties chose Must every day for years as he awoke at 5 a.m. to write stories about harrowing crimes and evil doings, all before going to his job at the courthouse.

Eventually, after three years of juggling writing and criminal defense, he shaped his stories into a novel, which he sent to publishers. Must is why, even as editors rejected his book again and again, the lawyer/author kept going and eventually received a yes, and it's why John Grisham is a household name today.

A small group of entrepreneurs in San Francisco chose Must when their new business idea—an unheard-of space rental service named AirbedAndBreakfast.com—was running out of money and the idea was not gaining traction. But because they believed it would succeed, the team hatched a wild idea: to create Airbnb-branded boxes of cereal and sell them at the 2008 Democratic National Convention.

The team designed a cartoon illustration of Obama, found a cereal manufacturer in California, hot glued the tops and numbered each one 1 through 500, and sold them online for $40 each as art. These collectable boxes ended up on CNN, *Good Morning America*, and across the press. "With hope in every bowl," the small fledgling Airbnb team found a creative way of making money fast when every conceivable metric said they *should* quit.

BUT IF

MUS

IS SO GREAT,

WE CHOOSE

EVERY

ST

WHY DON'T
T
DAY?

PART II

SHOULDS ARE PUT ON YOU FROM THE MOMENT YOU ARE BORN.

You have to grow up under someone else's wing. It's a normal, healthy process for parents to give Shoulds and for children to receive them. Because you—the child—must learn how to navigate the world. In addition to what you receive from your parents, you inherit a worldview from the community, culture, and specific time into which you are born. As you grow up, you get to decide how you feel about that worldview. It is a natural process to become your own person, to find your voice, convictions, and opinions, and to challenge and shed the Shoulds that no longer serve your evolving beliefs. But, sometimes, we linger in Should a little longer than expected.

Sometimes, a lot longer.

And we might even find ourselves as adults still living in a world of
Shoulds from childhood that we have not consciously examined.

"ARE YOU FAMILIAR WITH GURDJIEFF?"
ASKED A FRIEND. "HE WAS A
SPIRITUAL TEACHER AROUND THE
TURN OF THE CENTURY, AND ONE
DAY, HE POSED A QUESTION TO HIS
STUDENTS — 'IF A PRISONER WANTS
TO ESCAPE FROM PRISON, WHAT'S
THE FIRST THING HE NEEDS TO KNOW?'

'YOU NEED TO KNOW THE GUARD,' ONE
STUDENT SAID. 'YOU NEED TO FIND
THE KEY,' SAID ANOTHER.

'NO,' GURDJIEFF SAID, 'THE FIRST
THING THAT YOU NEED TO KNOW IF
YOU WANT TO ESCAPE FROM
PRISON IS THAT YOU ARE *IN*
PRISON. UNTIL YOU KNOW THAT,
NO ESCAPE IS POSSIBLE.'"

If you want to live the fullness of your life—if you want to be free—you must understand, first, why you are *not* free, what *keeps you* from being free. The word prison comes from the Latin *praehendere*, meaning to seize, grasp, capture. A prison doesn't have to be a physical place; it can be anything your mind creates. What has taken ahold of you? The natural process of socialization requires that the individual be influenced by Shoulds in order to function as a part of society. However, as you grow up, it is healthy to be self-aware about the Shoulds you inherited. You might value and keep some Shoulds, while others you might choose to discard.

If you want to know Must, get to know Should. This is hard work. *Really hard work.* We unconsciously imprison ourselves to avoid our most primal fears. We choose Should because choosing Must is terrifying, incomprehensible. Our prison is constructed from a lifetime of Shoulds, the world of choices we've unwittingly agreed to, the walls that alienate us from our truest, most authentic selves. Should is the doorkeeper to Must. And just as you create your prison, you can set yourself free.

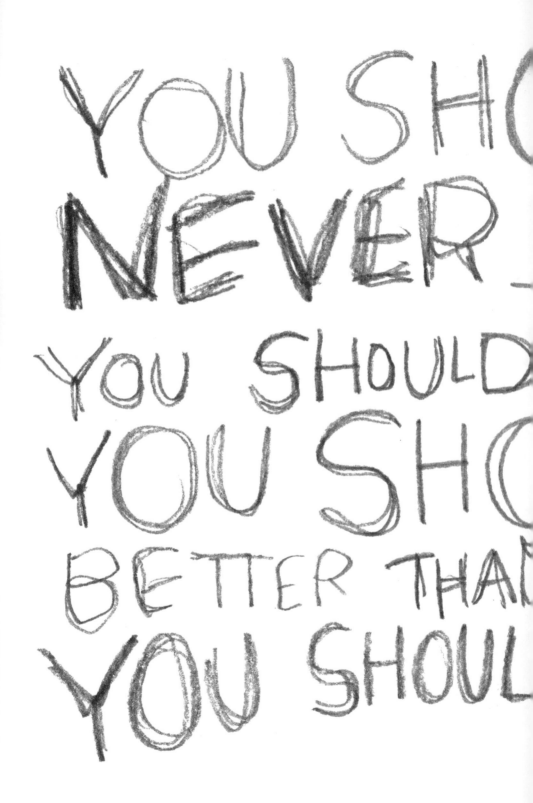

OULD

———————— .

ALWAYS———— .

ULD KNOW

TO ————— .

NOT————— .

HOW MIGHT WE REMOVE SHOULD FROM OUR LIVES?

Removing Should is hard and time-consuming. Because in order to remove it, we must first understand it, get to know it—*intimately*. We need to know each Should's origins, how it got there, and when we first began to integrate it into our decision-making. Look for recurring patterns, and choices—both little and big— that are affected. How often do we place blame on the person, job, or situation when the real problem, the real pain, is within us? And we leave and walk away, angry, frustrated, and sad, unconsciously carrying the same Shoulds into a new context— the next relationship, the next job, the next friendship—hoping for different results. But so long as we leave Should unexamined, the pattern repeats. And while running from Should certainly sounds easier and more pleasant, we must get to know Should if we want to release its invisible grip from our everyday decision-making.

If you're ready to get to know your Shoulds, you can. Here's one way.

Grab a piece of paper, and make a list of the Shoulds you hold on to by completing the sentences from the previous page. You can add more and repeat them if you want. Listen to what comes up first and write it down without thinking too much. Even if it doesn't make sense right now, it contains a grain of truth worth capturing.

Look at your list one by one, and ask the following three questions:

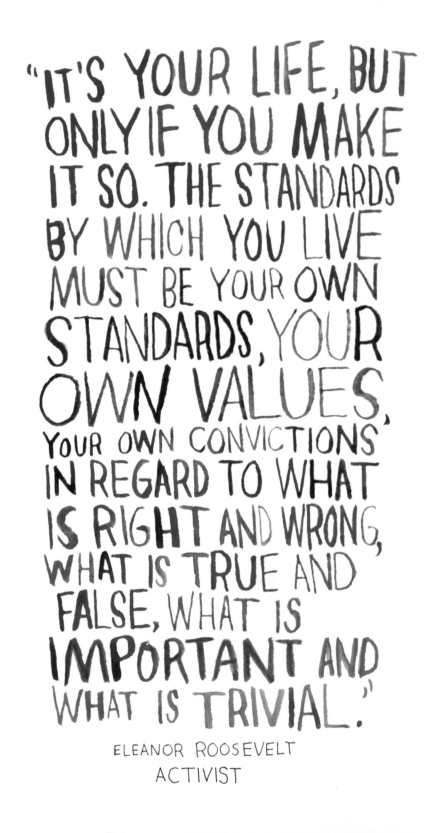

"IT'S YOUR LIFE, BUT ONLY IF YOU MAKE IT SO. THE STANDARDS BY WHICH YOU LIVE MUST BE YOUR OWN STANDARDS, YOUR OWN VALUES, YOUR OWN CONVICTIONS IN REGARD TO WHAT IS RIGHT AND WRONG, WHAT IS TRUE AND FALSE, WHAT IS IMPORTANT AND WHAT IS TRIVIAL."

ELEANOR ROOSEVELT
ACTIVIST

I've had help examining my Shoulds. Throughout my life, I have frequently felt that there was a heavy, lingering stigma surrounding counselors, therapists, and self-help. What was worse was when a person actually admitted *attending* therapy. It seemed to imply that there was something wrong with that person. This couldn't be further from the truth. Our cultural lack of encouragement for psychological health is one of the primary sources of our own unhappiness, dissatisfaction, and deepest inner suffering.

When you examine the Shoulds of your life, you are consciously choosing to get to know your prison—the expectations from other people's agendas, the belief systems you inhabit but don't truly embrace, and all the things you agreed to without realizing it. Shining a light on your list of Shoulds may involve facing some of your deepest fears, and finding support is wise. This is where the pros come in—therapists, counselors, and professionals who are trained to navigate this terrain. Working with a therapist in your day-to-day life is like having a trainer at the gym, except rather than work your muscles, the therapist works the organ that *thinks* it's running the show—your brain—and the source that's *really* running the show—your spirit.

There are also tools to help. The Enneagram is a powerful personality typology tool that empowers self-awareness. By better understanding yourself, you awaken to the patterns that you unconsciously repeat in your life. I even use the Enneagram *with* my therapist. Another effective tool is The Empty Chair Technique. It was developed in the 1940s as a part of Gestalt therapy. All you need are two chairs and fifteen minutes.

THE EMPTY CHAIR

Find a private room and place two chairs facing each other. Take a seat in one of them. The chairs may seem silly, but, trust me, it works better than doing it in your head.

The basic purpose of this exercise is to have a conversation with yourself. While you can use this technique for any topic, in this case, your Must and Should are going to talk to each other.

When you sit in the first chair, you are your Must—the part of you that has strong urges, convictions, intuition, and feelings. Sitting across from you is your own inner Should—the part of you that chooses to live your life in ways that are not congruent with your personal truth.

How do you feel looking at your own Should? Are you annoyed? Grateful? Mad as all hell? Do you have questions for Should? Ask away.

After you've said what you need to say, move to the other chair. Now, you are Should, and you are looking at Must. Respond to what you just heard. Answer Must's questions, defend yourself, get mad, yell, whatever it is—feel it all, express it to Must. When you're at a stopping point, stand up, switch chairs, and continue this back-and-forth dialogue. You'll know when to stop, and it can last as long or as short as you need, but try it for at least ten minutes to start.

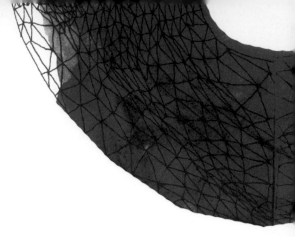

It's not easy to examine Should. It's painful, it takes time, and during the process, you might become vulnerable and irritable. You might even be able to notice when others are experiencing growing pains in life because they might close up, turn inward, and withdraw. This is normal because the process of transformation is exhausting.

The snake is the ancient sacred symbol for transformation. In order to grow, it must shed its skin. This process is painful, dangerous, and necessary for growth. The snake's insides are literally outgrowing its outsides, and it must remove its restrictive, outermost layer.

The snake rubs and scratches, feeling that something's not quite right. During the process, its coloring sometimes shifts to an indigo blue hue. If for some reason the snake cannot shed its skin, over time it will become malnourished, possibly even blind, and it will die from its inability to grow.

But when it successfully completes the process, the snake emerges stronger and healthier—a new incarnation.

This shape-shifting life cycle represents rebirth and renewal, the enigmatic power of life to thwart death. It is a metaphor for the experience that you, as an extraordinary human being capable of miraculous growth and transformation, have the opportunity to experience in your own life.

Siddhartha stood still and for a moment an icy chill stole over him. He shivered inwardly like a small animal, like a bird or a hare, when he realized how alone he was. He had been homeless for years and had not felt like this. Now he did feel it. Previously, when in deepest meditation, he was still his father's son, he was a Brahmin of high standing, a religious man. Now he was only Siddhartha, the awakened; otherwise nothing else. He breathed in deeply and for a moment he shuddered. Nobody was so alone as he. He was no nobleman, belonging to any aristocracy, no artisan belonging to any guild and finding refuge in it, sharing its life and language. . . . But he, Siddhartha, where did he belong? Whose life would he share? Whose language would he speak?

At that moment, when the world around him melted away, when he stood alone like a star in the heavens, he was overwhelmed by a feeling of icy despair, but he was more firmly himself than ever. That was the last shudder of his awakening, the last pains of birth. Immediately he moved on again and began to walk quickly and impatiently, no longer homewards, no longer to his father, no longer looking backwards.

HERMANN HESSE, *SIDDHARTHA*

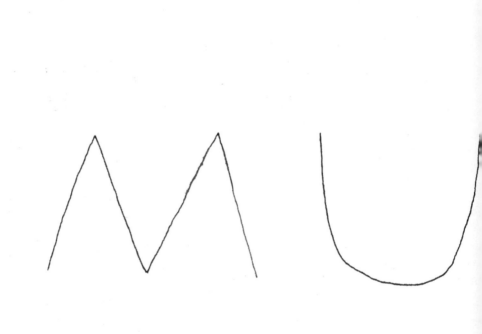

PART III

ST

THE PATH TO MUST IS A PATH
WE CREATE. IT BEGINS IN
PATHLESSNESS, NOTHINGNESS,
EMPTINESS— A TABULA RASA,
AS ARISTOTLE CALLED IT.

"If you can see your path laid out in front of you step by step, you know it's not your path," Joseph Campbell said. "Your own path you make with every step you take. That's why it's your path."

The tabula rasa is the blank page, a new roll of film, the pure canvas of white—unsullied, uncompromised. The term applies to more than just the objects of our creation; it is also a state of mind where nothing is scripted—a place where there is no map, no case study, and no right answer, and the only person who can decide what to do next is you.

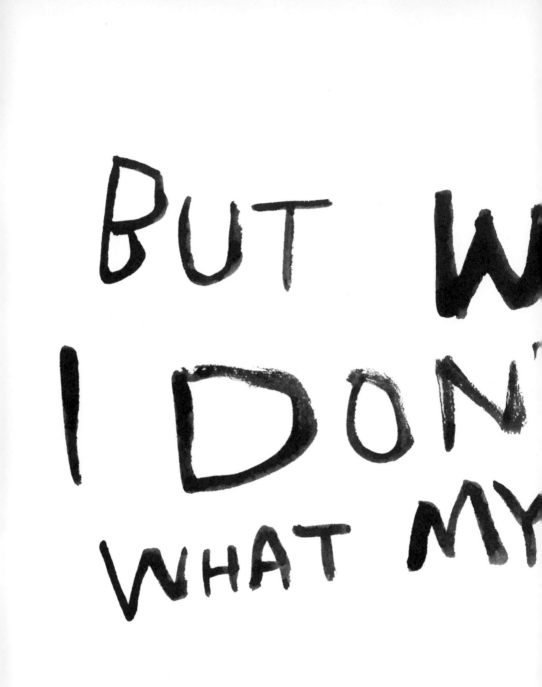

HAT IF

KNOW

MUST IS?

The very notion of having a calling—that you must have one—can be a nonstarter. It feels overwhelming.

HOW DO I FIND IT?

Daunting.

WHAT IF IT CHANGES OVER TIME?

Oppressive, even.

DOES EVERYBODY HAVE ONE?

Thinking that your Must will appear, fully formed, is like believing you can write a book by wishing and thinking. But doing one small thing, daily—*pick up the pen, write a paragraph, make a list of words*—that is how your Must will appear.

The following pages offer small activities that you can do in under ten minutes a day to begin to discover your Must.

Nowhere is the essence of Must more purely exhibited than in childhood.

What were you like as a child? What did you enjoy doing? Were you solitary or did you prefer a crowd? Independent or collaborative? Day optimizer or day dreamer?

If you don't remember, call your mom, or someone who knew you well in your early childhood, and ask for stories about what you were like as a kid. Take notes on a piece of paper and hold on to them. These stories hold the earliest seeds of your Must.

LOOK WITHIN

Must is always with you, wherever you are, whatever you're doing. Must *is* you. Sometimes, Must can feel really far away, but it will never leave you. You just might not see it yet.

IF YOU HAD ONE DAY TO PURSUE SOME IDEA, ACTIVITY, OR PROJECT, WHAT ARE THREE THINGS THAT COME TO MIND FIRST?

THINGS YOU DO JUST FOR FUN:

SOMETHING A FRIEND DOES THAT YOU FEEL ENVIOUS ABOUT:

THINGS
YOU DO WHEN
YOU'RE PROCRASTINATING

FANTASIES

AN ACTIVITY
THAT GIVES YOU CHILLS:

SIGHTS, SMELLS, SOUNDS, OR
SENSATIONS THAT GIVE YOU
BUTTERFLIES IN YOUR STOMACH...

WRITE YOUR OBITUARY

THE TWO OBITUARIES

Roz Savage was thirty-three, a management consultant, living "the big life" in London, when she sat down and wrote two versions of her obituary:

> The first was the life that I wanted to have. I thought of the obituaries that I enjoyed reading, the people that I admired . . . the people [who] really knew how to live. The second version was the obituary that I was heading for—a conventional, ordinary, pleasant life. The difference between the two was startling. Clearly something was going to have to change. . . . I felt I was getting a few things figured out. But I was like a carpenter with a brand-new set of tools and no wood to work on. I needed a project. And so I decided to row the Atlantic.

Write two versions of your obituary on two pieces of paper. Don't worry about being overly practical. Consider how your life will progress along the path it's on. And then consider what might be written if you heed your call.

ACQUIRE ONE NEW SKILL A MONTH

Every month, choose one new thing to do:

GO SWIMMING

LEARN ABOUT SAKE

DO HEADSTANDS

Your activities might appear to be unrelated, but over time, your interests will integrate and cross-pollinate because they have one common element—you. As designer Charles Eames was fond of saying, "Eventually everything connects." And it will.

As you try new activities, take notes in a dedicated place—a notebook, notecards, or on your computer.

LOOK FOR PATTERNS

Hang up all of your pieces of paper—notes, lists, obituaries, and skills acquired. Put them in a place where the collection can grow and you can see everything all at once.

Look for patterns, connections, and recurring themes. Prefer to work in pairs? Hate sitting all day? Find sensory stimulation important for your process? Take note when connections begin to happen between seemingly disparate activities. As new ideas pop up, add them. As hypotheses emerge, grab them. Then go out and experiment and play with what you're learning. Share your insights with trusted peers. Integrate their feedback and repeat until you start to home in on your Must.

CURRENT OBITUARY 1

OBITUARY 2

NEW SKILLS

THINGS I ENJOYED DOING AS A KID

CRAZY WILD FANTASIES & DREAMS

ACTIVITIES THAT GIVE ME THE CHILLS:

ONE DAY EXPLORATION ACTIVITIES:

WOOD CARVING

SPEED READING

COOKING

GIVING MORE HUGS

SPORTS CAR RACING

DRAWING

RESEARCHING

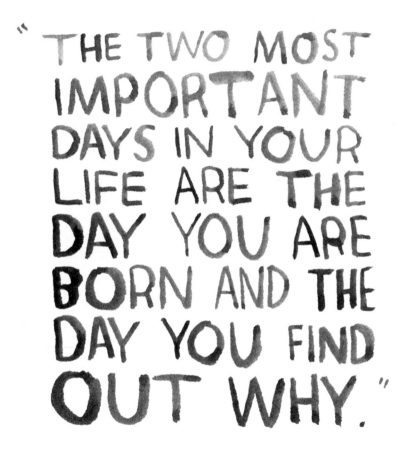

"THE TWO MOST IMPORTANT DAYS IN YOUR LIFE ARE THE DAY YOU ARE BORN AND THE DAY YOU FIND OUT WHY."

MARK TWAIN
AUTHOR

Must eludes you because once you hear it speak, once you know what it is and what it wants—to teach . . . to build a family . . . to write . . . to make art . . . to put people on the moon—it is difficult, if not impossible, to forget it. When you know why you are here—what you were put on this earth to do—it is challenging to go back to life as you knew it and be satisfied. And this is why Must is elusive. This is why we avoid admitting what we want. This is why our deepest desires sit in hiding for months, years, a lifetime. And this is why this journey is fascinating, intoxicating, and downright intimidating.

WRITE DOWN YOUR MUST

On a card. On a newspaper. On a napkin or an expired bus ticket. And then . . .

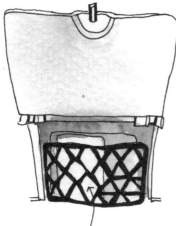

LEAVE IT ON
AN AIRPLANE

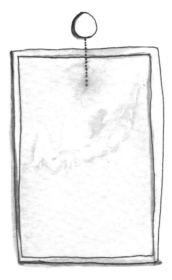

WRITE IT ON THE
BATHROOM MIRROR

WRITE IT ON THE
BOTTOM OF YOUR
SHOES

BLOW IT UP

SEND IT TO
SOMEONE

ATTACH IT TO A
BALLOON

WHISPER IT
TO A BUG

PIN IT TO A COFFEE
SHOP BULLETIN BOARD

MAKE IT YOUR
SCREEN SAVER

BURY IT

STITCH IT INSIDE YOUR BAG

A MUSICIAN
MUSIC, AN A
PAINT, A
MUST WI
IS TO BE
AT PEACE
WHAT A
HE MUS

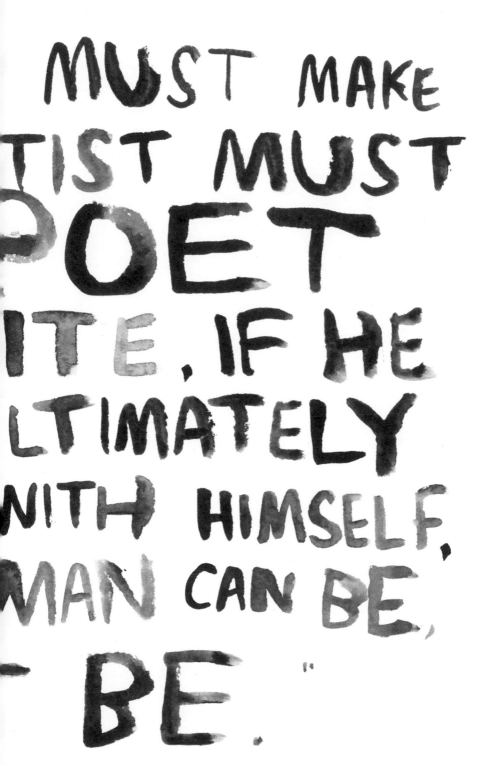

MUST MAKE
TIST MUST
POET
ITE, IF HE
LTIMATELY
WITH HIMSELF,
MAN CAN BE,
BE."

ABRAHAM MASLOW
PSYCHOLOGIST

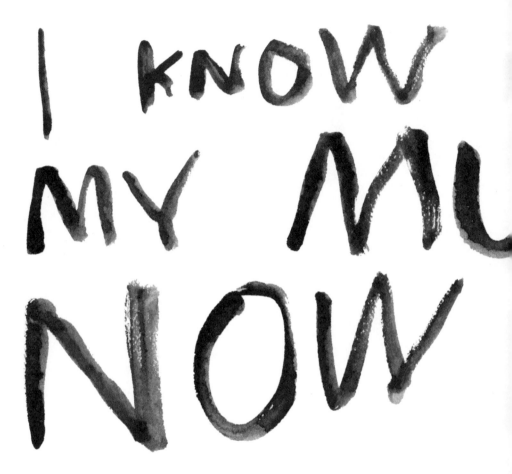

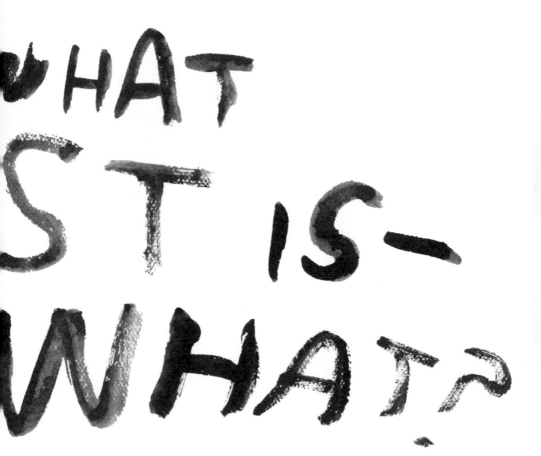

When we discover our Must, the brain's most primal, protective center gets alarmed. The riot gear is called forth. Defense mechanisms go up. Because choosing Must raises very real and scary questions.

Let's get practical.

There are four big concerns people have about achieving a sustainable Must. The first is Money.

MONEY

WHAT IF DOING WHAT I LOVE DOESN'T PAY?

If you want to get by on this planet, you must make money.
If you have obligations or a family or a mortgage, you must make more money. If doing what you love doesn't pay the bills, then you must find another way to make money. Period. Being able to pay your bills can create the temporal and mental space to find your calling.

A JOB   A CAREER   A CALLING

The author T. S. Eliot was also a banker. Another writer, Kurt Vonnegut, sold cars. One of the greatest composers of our time, Philip Glass, didn't earn a living from his calling making music until he was forty-two. Even as his work was premiering at the Met, he worked as a plumber and renewed his taxi license, just in case.

You might have a nine-to-five job while you pursue your calling on nights and weekends. Or you might focus on your calling full-time and make a living from it. There are many options to choose from, and there is dignity in all work. Just because you have a job to pay the bills does not make it dirty. And just because you want to find your calling does not mean you need to quit your job. You get to play with these three types of work and decide what's right for you and your life.

Albert Einstein struggled for almost two years to find work after college, until a friend offered him a desk job reviewing patents inside a room with a window overlooking a cloister. In his biography of Einstein, Walter Isaacson writes: "He came to believe that it was a benefit to his science, rather than a burden, to work instead in 'that worldly cloister where I hatched my most beautiful ideas.'"

Return to p.42

So long as you keep your eye on your Must and optimize your time and energy to sustain it as best you can, you can continue to adjust and experiment with how you make money.

Maybe you'll get paid to do what you love. Or maybe you'll take a job where the hours are clearly defined, the work isn't too exhausting, and you have energy to pursue your Must on nights and weekends.

But what you don't want is to take a job that was intended to pay the bills and suddenly, you don't have time to explore your passion, you're too tired to step into that which you were put on this earth to do. And if, for some awful reason, you forget that money is a game, a make-believe concept that some people invented, you could be led back into the complex layered world of Should. And here, the loss isn't a financial one. *You* are the cost. Is it worth it?

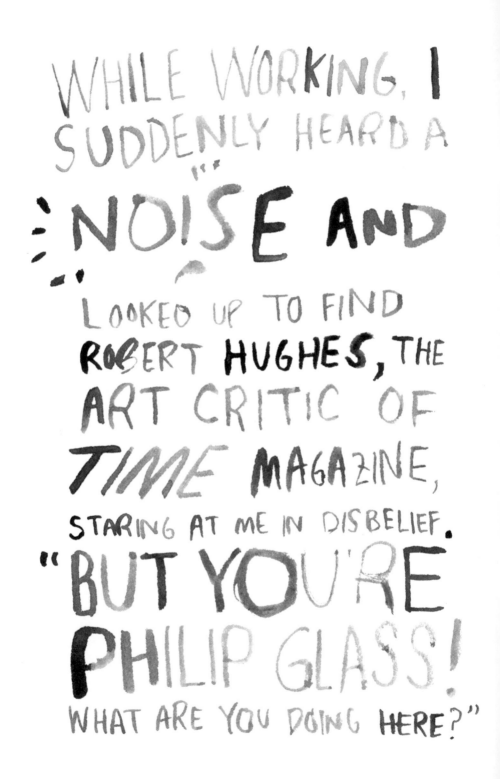

IT WAS OBVIOUS THAT I WAS INSTALLING HIS DISHWASHER, AND I TOLD HIM I WOULD SOON BE FINISHED. "BUT YOU ARE AN ARTIST," HE PROTESTED. I EXPLAINED THAT I WAS AN ARTIST BUT THAT I WAS SOMETIMES A PLUMBER AS WELL AND THAT HE SHOULD GO AWAY AND LET ME FINISH.

PHILIP GLASS
COMPOSER

HOW MUCH MONEY IS ENOUGH MONEY?

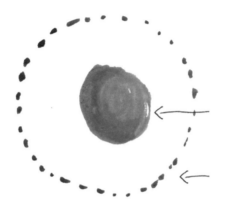

Must-Have Money

Nice-to-Have Money

There are two types of money—Must-Have and Nice-to-Have. Must-Have money is a solid, fixed number that we do not want to risk not having. We will not be able to focus on our Must if we are worried about not being able to eat. This number is often smaller than you might assume. At its most basic, it includes food and shelter.

Nice-to-Have Money is extra, above-and-beyond money. Too often, we confuse Nice-to-Have money with Must-Have. Just because something is valuable doesn't mean that we need it. It will always be nicer to have more Nice-to-Have money.

What are the things that you must have to live? What about things that are nice to have? Is a car nice to have or a must-have? A safer place to live? More frequent, considered life experiences? Supporting your family? Paying off loans? A bus pass? Child care? Prototypes for your new idea? A space to work?

Beyond the absolutes, money is a game, and you can play it any way you want.

When a man is warmed . . . what does he want next? Surely not more warmth of the same kind, as more and richer food, larger and more splendid houses, finer and more abundant clothing, more numerous incessant and hotter fires, and the like. When he has obtained those things which are necessary to life, there is another alternative than to obtain the superfluities; and that is, to adventure on life now, his vacation from humbler toil having commenced.

HENRY DAVID THOREAU, *WALDEN*

WILL CHOOSING MUST MAKE ME RICH?

YES.

The wealthiest people I know have days and nights filled with life's most priceless items:

WATCHING THE
SUN RISE

SMELLING
THE RAIN

MAKING
SCRAMBLED EGGS
ON A WEEKDAY

MAKING IT TO YOUR
FAVORITE EXERCISE CLASS

HAVING BELLY LAUGHS WITH A FRIEND

KISSING

MAKING TEA
BEFORE BED

MAKING A MEAL
FOR SOMEONE
SPECIAL

WRITING A
HANDWRITTEN NOTE

WALKING SLOWLY
ENOUGH TO SMELL
THE FLOWERS

EATING AN
ICE CREAM
SANDWICH

TAKING A
POINTLESS BIKE RIDE

REMEMBERING
ALL YOUR DREAMS

READING THE
SUNDAY FUNNIES

TAKING THE LONG
WAY HOME

GOING ON A
WALKING
MEETING

Time is the second perceived stumbling block to Must.

"I'LL MAKE TIME AFTER THINGS SETTLE DOWN AT THE OFFICE..."

"...WHEN THE KIDS ARE OFF TO TO SCHOOL..."

You make time for what you want.

If you're not prioritizing the things you say you care about, consider the possibility that you don't actually care about those things. Often, knowing what we want is the hardest part. What do you want? Do you know?

I once attended a dinner party where guests were invited to write down their wildest, craziest dreams on notecards. These were the kinds of dreams that you rarely admitted because you wanted them not just a little bit or kind of, but deeply, murderously, sacrilegiously.

I listened to people share their audacious dreams, their *terrifying* dreams. And when it was my turn to share, I looked at my cards and saw a lifeless, wilting collection of boring dreams that I couldn't have cared less about.

I went home, pinned my boring dreams on the wall next to my bed, and got serious about making them better. Getting to know what I wanted required heightened sensitivity, and it started by staying alert to my urges and wants—little and big. This heightened my intuition and connected me to that little voice in my head that wants things—crazy things, silly things, dirty things, quiet things. The more I fed it, the louder it spoke. Cards spilled into the bathroom, above the kitchen sink. Wants fell out of coat pockets and into other people's purses. It turns out that the more intimate we are with what we want, the more self-aware we will be about how we spend our time.

SWIM IN SALT WATER

PAINT A

LEARN TO SHOOT A
BOW & ARROW

LEARN T

HIKE TO ANNAPURNA
BASE CAMP

PLAY TH

"I HAVE AN AMBITION
TO LIVE 300 YEARS.
I WILL NOT LIVE 300 YEARS.
MAYBE I WILL LIVE ONE YEAR
MORE. BUT I HAVE THE
AMBITION. WHY YOU WILL
NOT HAVE AMBITION? WHY?
HAVE THE GREATEST
AMBITION POSSIBLE. YOU
WANT TO BE IMMORTAL? FIGHT
TO BE IMMORTAL. DO IT.
YOU WANT TO MAKE THE
MOST FANTASTIC ART OR
MOVIE? TRY. IF YOU FAIL,
IS NOT IMPORTANT. WE
NEED TO TRY."

ALEJANDRO JODOROWSKY
CHILEAN FRENCH FILMMAKER

"BUT I HAVE FIVE KIDS AND A MORTGAGE."

We all have a net of obligations and time constraints—both real and imagined. The most effective way to find your Must is to find ten minutes. Because while running away from all of your obligations to focus uninterrupted on your Must for months sounds romantic, the harder, trickier, and more sustainable way is to make shifts every day within your existing reality. To integrate, not obliterate.

Finding pockets of time for your Must is a daily effort. And once you have that pocket of time, move from thinking about your Must to doing something about it. Ten minutes can be found all over the place:

Ten minutes for the tea kettle to boil—GO!

Ten minutes while you wait for your laundry to dry—GO!

Ten minutes of commercials during half an hour of TV—GO!

Ten minutes waiting in the carpool lane—GO!

Time, which could have been a limitation, becomes a gift.

"BUT I'M PAST

TWENTIES

Husband and wife duo Ryan and Tina Essmaker were in their twenties when they started an online publication titled *The Great Discontent*. After three years, they quit their day jobs and turned their part-time passion into a globally distributed print magazine featuring interviews on beginnings, creativity, and risk.

THIRTIES

Leonard Cohen was a struggling poet until he traveled to New York to make music. He gave his first major performance at the age of thirty-three.

FORTIES

Chef Julia Child wandered until she found her calling in food. *Mastering the Art of French Cooking* was published when she was forty-nine. "Really, the more I cook the more I like to cook," she wrote to her sister-in-law. "To think it has taken me 40 yrs. to find my true passion (cat and husb. excepted)."

FIFTIES

After traveling to Bali and seeing the disrepair of many 100-year-old Javanese houses called *joglos*, Argentinean architect Alejandra Cisneros used her expertise in sustainable architecture to reclaim, rebuild, and repair the culturally significant structures. With respect and thoughtfulness, Alejandra and her small team are supporting the culture, one *joglo* at a time.

MY PRIME."

SIXTIES

Laura Ingalls Wilder, author of the *Little House on the Prairie* series, published *Little House in the Big Woods*, her first book, at the age of sixty-four.

SEVENTIES

John Glenn became the oldest person to go into space at the age of seventy-seven.

EIGHTIES

When she was 81, Ginette Bedard ran her twelfth consecutive New York City Marathon. She started running at the age of 69. Of running marathons, she has said, "I'm going to do this until destiny takes me away."

NINETIES

International design firm IDEO hired a ninety-year-old designer.

HUNDREDS

Grandma Moses, as Anna Mary Robertson Moses was called, produced over one thousand paintings in the last thirty years of her life after her arthritis made it impossible for her to crochet. She picked up a paintbrush, and at the age of one hundred, she was featured on the cover of *Time* magazine.

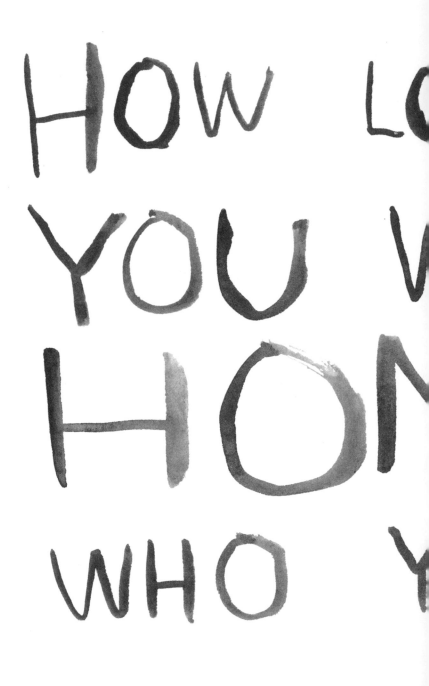

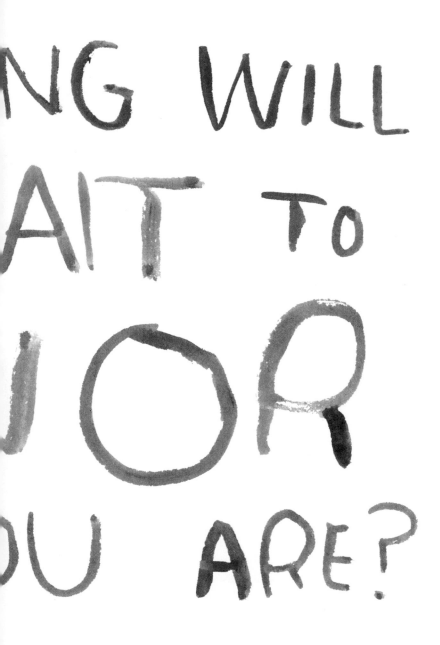

"BUT I DON'T HAVE SPACE FOR MUST."

Space is the third stumbling block to finding your Must.

You may think you don't have space for Must because you don't have an office or a studio or even a door. While you do need a physical space, it could be a desk at the public library, a garden bench, or, if you're my friend Sharon, a space that you create using a $4.99 roll of painter's tape.

"I needed my own work space," she said as we walked through her home, "so I did this." Running along the floor, up the wall, across the ceiling and back down again, painter's tape marked off a sliver of space next to her living room. On the other side of that tape, Sharon had placed a narrow desk against the wall. Her tools were neatly arranged. "Inspiration" was pinned above the desk. The space was inspired and intimate. Repeatedly written on the tape in neat handwriting were the words "No Judgment Zone."

Another friend, a busy mom of two, once shared with me her practice of lighting a candle to mark the beginning of her daily ritual time. When the kids went down for a nap, she would tuck away and use that time to read, write, and reconnect. This space is both physical and emotional. It's a place to think. A place to be. A place to quiet the world and connect to the currents within. And at the end of this time, she blows the candle out.

You need a physical space—private, safe, and just for you. When you are in this space, you are not available. I repeat, *you are not available*. This is your sacred space to be by and with yourself. We all need safe containers. How might you create a safe space that you can spend time in daily? How might you get creative with where it begins and ends? Find this place and make it your own.

PLAY IN YOUR SPACE!

Must loves play. Play is messy, chaotic even. Things get flipped upside down and inside out and torn up and pulled apart and put back together again in new combinations. This is where doors open into unforeseen worlds. What would happen if you wrote with your left hand? Your toes? Or your leftovers from dinner? Play opens up possibility. And an effective way to keep tuned in to that playful spirit is to build a collection of unconventional tools. When you're stuck, when you need a jolt, when you crave to see things from a new perspective, it's time to play. You don't have to be a painter to use a paintbrush or a carpenter to use a hammer. When you play with new tools and methods, you will literally activate parts of your mind that have become hard to reach over time.

An incomplete list of potential tools you can play with:

PHOTO COPIERS   PENCILS   MARKERS   BRUSHES   YOUR TOES

PIZZA SAUCE   SUNLIGHT   FIRE   DIRT   LEAVES

SPRAY PAINT   DISSASSEMBLED ELECTRONICS   MASKS   BUBBLES

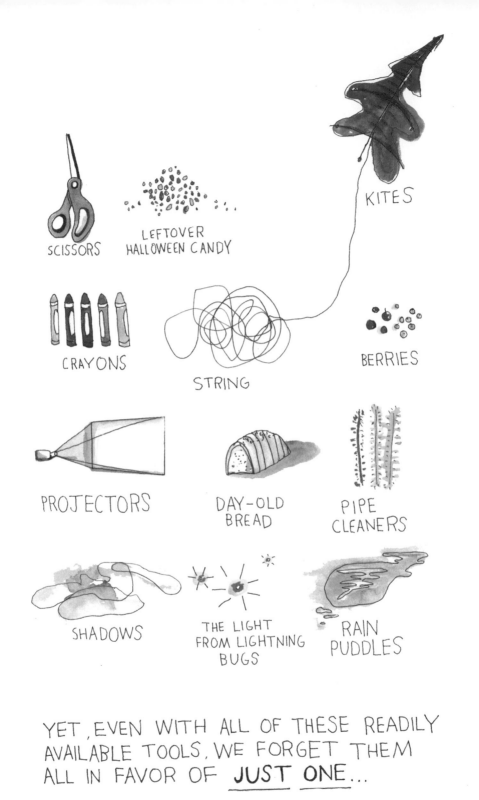

SCISSORS

LEFTOVER HALLOWEEN CANDY

KITES

CRAYONS

STRING

BERRIES

PROJECTORS

DAY-OLD BREAD

PIPE CLEANERS

SHADOWS

THE LIGHT FROM LIGHTNING BUGS

RAIN PUDDLES

YET, EVEN WITH ALL OF THESE READILY AVAILABLE TOOLS, WE FORGET THEM ALL IN FAVOR OF **JUST ONE**...

The computer is a powerful tool, but it is overemphasized when it comes to making. As Paul Rand, the father of graphic design in America, writes in his manifesto, *Design, Form, and Chaos*:

> *The language of the computer is the language of technology . . .*
> *of production. It enters the world of creativity only as an adjunct, as*
> *a tool—a time-saving device, a means of investigating, retrieving, and*
> *executing tedious jobs—but not as the principal player.*

Fill your tool kit with objects that inspire you to see in new ways.

SLAM FLASH HEY! !
PPPPPPSSSSS HEY !
SpAM

YOU NEED
PSYCHOLOGICAL
SPACE.

SLAM BEEP   BEEP
BEEP BEEP BEEP
BEEP BEEP BEEP
BEEP

Must needs solitude.

Solitude is how we quiet the voices, the incessant chatter. It's how we create the necessary calm, empty spaces. Vision needs solitude. Leadership needs solitude. Courage needs solitude. Because when our choices evolve from an internal place of sure-footed, rooted knowing, we become resilient, emboldened, and focused.

When was the last time you were alone with yourself? What was it like? How does the idea of having solitude—whether for one hour or for one month—make you feel?

Integrating solitude into our lives must be done in sustainable, everyday ways. Here are a few ideas:

WASH THE DISHES

SIT IN A CHURCH
DURING OFF-HOURS

SWEEP THE FLOORS
EVERY MORNING

WATCH THE
MOON RISE

MEDITATE

TAKE A WALK AT THE
END OF THE DAY — ALONE

SET A TIMER FOR
THIRTY MINUTES
AND DO NOT CHECK
YOUR PHONE

SIT QUIETLY WITH
A FRIEND

PLANT A GARDEN

REST

TAKE THREE
DEEP BREATHS

SLEEP IN NATURE
WITHOUT TECHNOLOGY

WASH A HEAD OF
LETTUCE LEAF BY LEAF

TAKE TIME EACH DAY
TO FEEL THE SUN
AGAINST YOUR FACE

While money, time, and space are the reasons given most often for not choosing Must, there's another fear that's far scarier and spoken about much less.

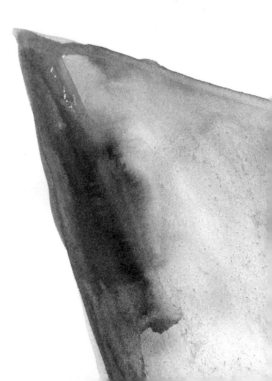

VULNERABILITY

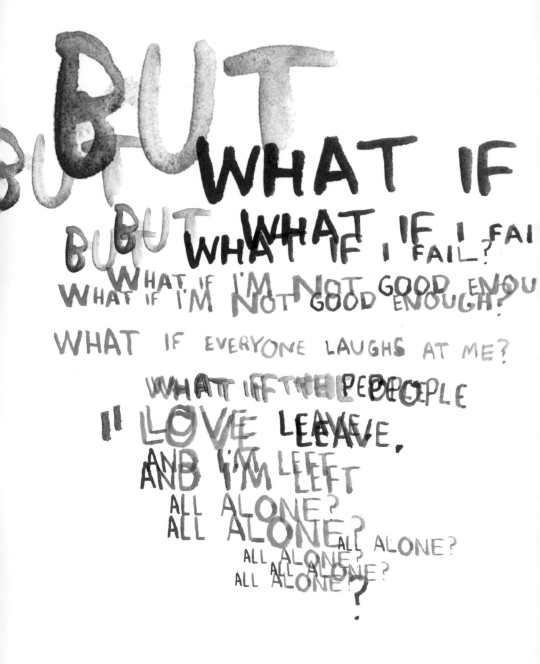

Choosing Must means that you have to confront some very big fears. It will make you feel vulnerable.

You might find yourself wondering if people you love will leave, if places will no longer feel the same, or if you will be all alone. You might ask what it's all for. Some obscure dream? A childhood fantasy? A fleeting feeling that you can't even really understand or explain?

It is here, standing at the crossroads of Should and Must, that we feel the enormous reality of our fears, and this is the moment when many of us decide against following our intuition, turning away from that place where nothing is guaranteed, nothing is known, and everything is possible.

THE WHAT-ARE-YOU-SO-AFRAID-OF LIST

Grab a piece of paper and write the numbers one through ten on the left side of the page. At the top, title it "What are you so afraid of?" This is your worst-case scenario list. This is your list of fears, ultimate doomsday concerns, and everyone-is-going-to-laugh-at-me-and-run-the-other-way scenarios. These are your largest, scariest fears, and you've got ten minutes to write them down.

Go.

Now let's get realistic about these fears. Because often, fears in our mind can be like sap—sticky and very difficult to remove. But fears on paper? Tangible. Visible. Cross-out-able.

Line by line, walk yourself through each of your fears. Examine them. Bring them into light. Is this fear a realistic one? Is it worth designing your life around? Or is it more of an emotional fear? Something to be mindful about as you move forward? Have a conversation with yourself about each one.

After you've gone through all of your fears, write a short note or tip next to each line listing one thing—just one—that you can do to loosen that fear's grip on your life. Get to know these fears intimately because they are the invisible walls that surround you daily. Decide which ones stay and which ones gotta go.

1.
2.
3.
4.
5.
6.
7.
8.
9.
10.

YOU MUST BEGIN

A journey of a thousand miles begins with a single step.

LAO-TZU

To choose Must requires action. You must do something. It is the small big moment that can take days, years, perhaps a lifetime to begin. And when you're ready, you choose it by doing something—anything—regardless if it's big or small. And just like that, you're on the road to Must.

To choose Must is to:

WRITE THAT
.IDE A DOWN

ASK THAT
QUESTION

GRAB THAT COFFEE

LISTEN TO
THAT SONG

BOOK THAT TRIP

LAY OUT
THE TOOLS

BRAINSTORM ON THAT TOPIC

BLOCK OFF THIRTY
MINUTES TO DO
THAT THING YOU'VE
BEEN PUTTING OFF

MAKE THAT
FIRST MARK

HAVE THAT CONVERSATION

LAY OUT THOSE
COLORS

FIND THAT OLD
BOX IN STORAGE

CLEAR OFF THE DESK

OPEN TO A BLANK PAGE &
COMMIT TO WRITING
FOR FIFTEEN MINUTES

PLAY ONE
CHORD

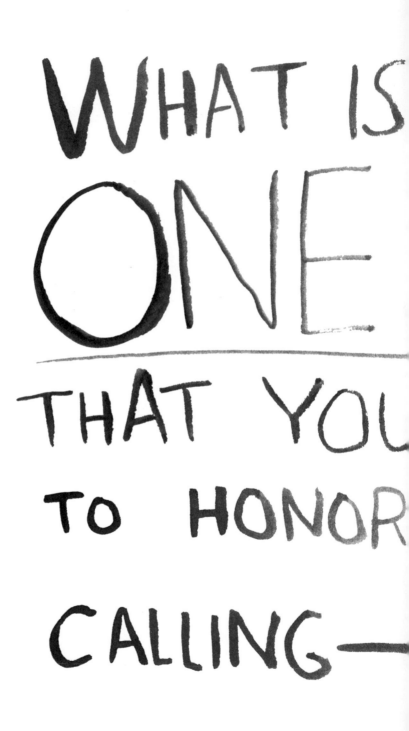

WHAT IS ONE THAT YOU TO HONOR CALLING—

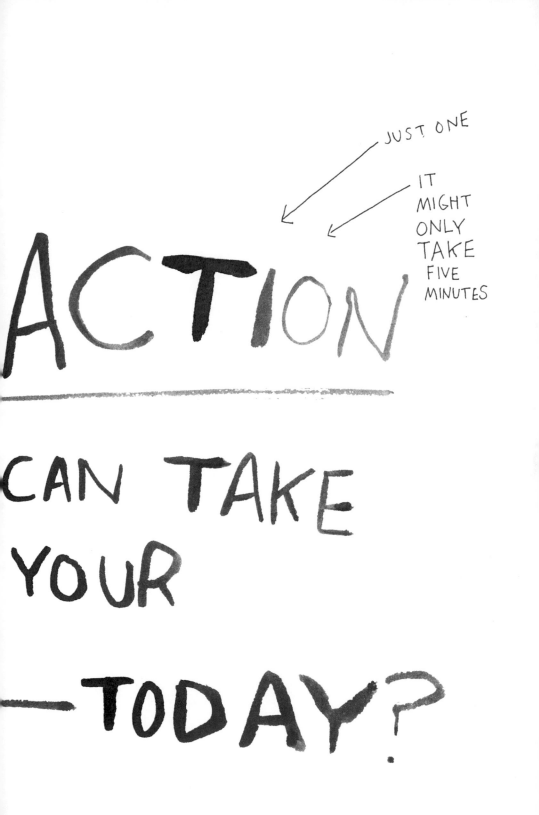

If you find yourself peering over the edge of an enormous cliff where you can't see anything down below, back up.

DON'T MAKE THE LEAP !!!

While this journey asks that you surrender to the unknown, it does not ask you to put yourself—or those around you—at risk. To choose Must is not like Evel Knievel proclaiming he will do the unthinkable. It is not a spectator sport. Must is too important, *way too important*, to be chosen on a whim, out of excitement, out of intoxication. That kind of decision-making is certain death.

The most sustainable Musts happen slowly, thoughtfully, and quietly. They don't happen impulsively but are built with a sober, calm intention.

Every decision you make counts. Ten minutes of solitude. One Must instead of one Should. Setting up your space. Writing your wants down and pinning them to the wall. Must is not a faraway land that you hope to arrive at sometime in the future, it's not for tomorrow or another day. Must is for today, now. And as you take daily action, the cliff will cease to be a cliff. It will simply become an obvious next step along your path to Must.

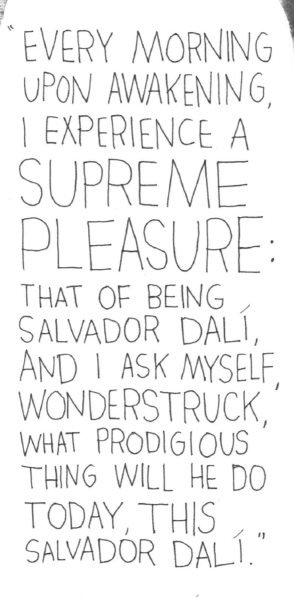

"EVERY MORNING UPON AWAKENING, I EXPERIENCE A SUPREME PLEASURE: THAT OF BEING SALVADOR DALÍ, AND I ASK MYSELF, WONDERSTRUCK, WHAT PRODIGIOUS THING WILL HE DO TODAY, THIS SALVADOR DALÍ."

SALVADOR DALÍ

PAINTER

SO NOW WHAT?
JUST GET UP AND
WORK EVERY DAY?

YES.

ALONE?

MOST LIKELY.

FOR WHAT?

UNCLEAR.

FOR WHOM?

YOURSELF.

FOR HOW LONG?

NO ONE KNOWS.

WHY?

BECAUSE YOU'VE GOT TO.

BUT WHAT IF I FAIL?

YOU WILL.

AND THEN WHAT?

YOU GET TO DECIDE IF YOU KEEP DOING THIS.

IS THIS A BAD IDEA?

THERE'S NO SUCH THING.

BUT WHAT IF IT'S HORRIBLE?

STOP DOUBTING. START DOING.

WILL WE HAVE THIS CONVERSATION AGAIN TOMORROW?

IF YOU WISH.

WHERE DOES IT ALL LEAD?

GRAB THE NEAREST TOOL. WORK.
AND IN TIME, YOU WILL KNOW.

PART IV

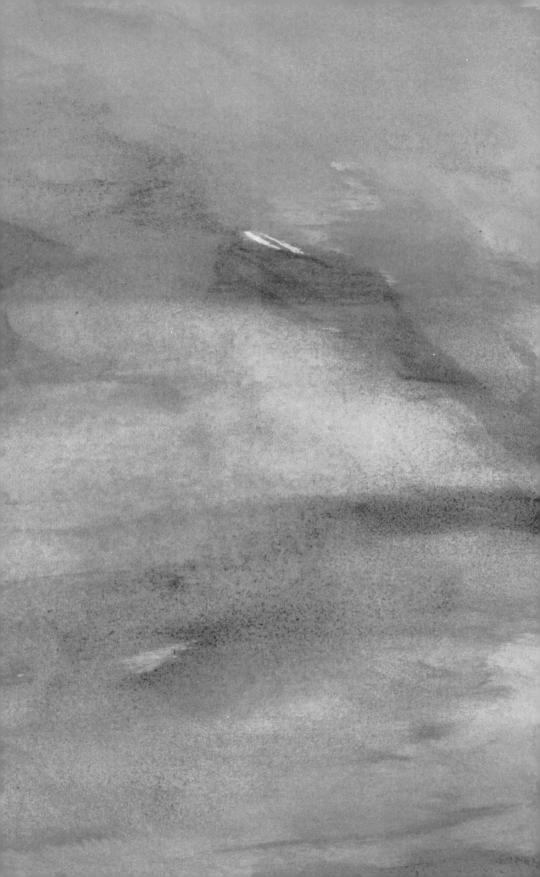

MUST IS A CHOICE YOU MAKE EVERY SINGLE DAY. TODAY. TOMORROW. AGAIN AND AGAIN. MUST.

It is constant effort and hard work—and inexplicably life-affirming—to honor who you are, what you believe, and why you are here. To choose Must is the greatest thing you can do with your life because this congruent, rooted way of living shines through *everything* that you do. Your sacred space and daily efforts will become even more sacred. You will build a beautiful world for your Must. And over time, it will be tempting to stay forever in this magical place that you've created, never to return to the everyday world again. But the complete and ultimate journey requires that you return, share your Must, and in so doing, lift the lives of others.

" IT'S NOT
ENOUGH TO
REACH THE
TREASURE,
ONE MUST
BRING IT
BACK. "

ROGER LIPSEY
AUTHOR

ME&WE

After building apps and websites that were available on phones anywhere for anyone, I couldn't shake the feeling of solitariness that I had about making art. Unlike design, painting didn't involve user research, and there was no target audience to keep in mind. It was just me, in a room, alone, making art. My concern grew.

WHEN DOES THIS INTERSECT WITH THE REST OF THE WORLD?

Must feels inherently selfish at first. But when you choose Must, you inspire others to choose it, too. When you follow Must every day, you impact not only what you create for your work, but also who you become in your life. This is how your work and your life become one and the same. When you choose Must, what you create *is* yourself. It is a *body* of work. As you change, so too does the work. As you grow, so too does the creation. Your work lives and breathes because you live and breathe. When you live the fullness of your life, you lift the collective human experience. As William Blake wrote, "Everything that lives, lives not alone nor for itself." Here, there is no longer a divide between you and others or giving and receiving. It is all one and the same, a fluid dance, a constant conversation where we can no longer tell where one ends and the other begins.

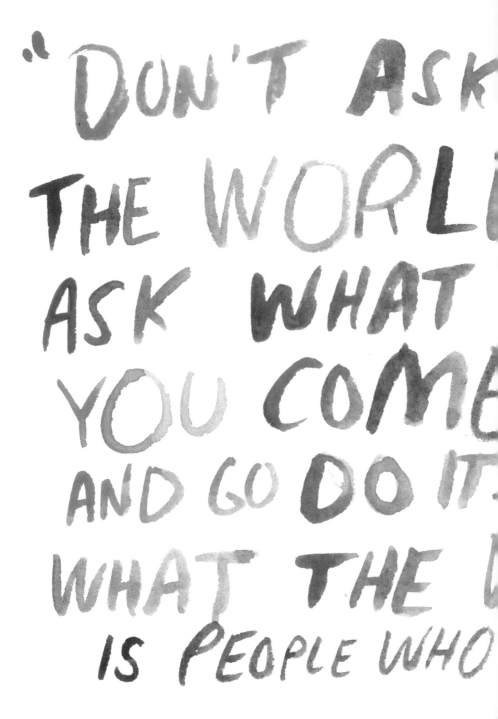

"DON'T ASK
THE WORLD
ASK WHAT
YOU COME
AND GO DO IT.
WHAT THE
IS PEOPLE WHO

HOWARD THURM

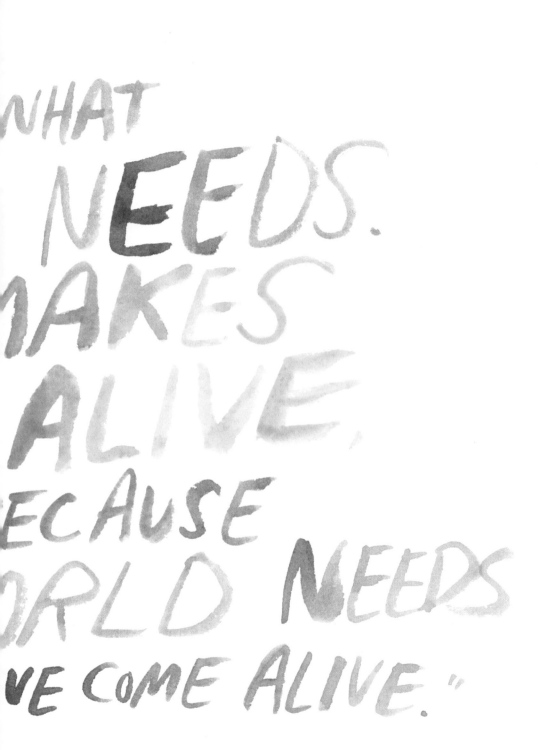

"WHAT NEEDS. MAKES ALIVE. ECAUSE ORLD NEEDS VE COME ALIVE."

LOSOPHER

HOW WILL YOU CONNECT WITH OTHERS—WITH YOUR WORK, AND YOUR LIFE?

START A BLOG

POST A PHOTO TO INSTAGRAM

LEAVE STORIES ON THE BUS

VOLUNTEER

WORK WITH KIDS

WRITE MESSAGES ON SIDEWALKS WITH CHALK

PAINT ART ON FOUND OBJECTS

MAKE TEMPORARY
TATTOOS

SHARE YOUR THOUGHTS
WITH OTHER PEOPLE

MENTOR/TUTOR

WRITE AN ESSAY

BEGIN A WEEKLY
CALL WITH LIKE-
MINDED PEOPLE

JOIN OR START
A BOOK CLUB

PUT UP WHEATPASTE POSTERS IN PUBLIC

START A SPECIAL-INTEREST
GROUP AT WORK

RIPPLES

As you choose Must, your actions affect everyone and everything around you.

How will you inspire others? Will you even know? Will it be because they see your work? Read your papers? Delight in your products? Or will it be because of that way you listen to them when they speak? How warmly you hug? How you live as you move through your days? Will it be something you say? Or some way that you say it? Or will it be the resounding peace that words cannot express? Although you might not be able to see the impact your life is having, it is there, under the surface, on another plane that we can feel but perhaps not see.

Have you ever been to northern California and stood at the base of a redwood tree? If you have, you know firsthand its majesty, its size, the trunk that you and even two or three friends cannot wrap your arms around. These trees reach unfathomable heights, strong and beautiful, lifting skyward. But what you cannot see when you stand at the foot of this tree is what is happening underneath. While a redwood tree can grow 360 feet tall, the roots are only, on average, about ten feet deep. This is because they spread their roots outward, searching for other redwood trees. Their roots intertwine under the ground, and they hold each other up. A redwood tree cannot stand on its own, and neither can we. The source of Must connects us all.

To act is to modify the shape of the world.

JEAN-PAUL SARTRE

A PLACE BEYOND

We can't prove Must. We can't point to it, or define where it stops and starts, because it's not a thing that we can see. But we know that it exists because when it's near, we feel it in our gut; it begs for a second glance, pulls us into another dimension, a space out of time where a day can pass in a moment.

"When it is working, you completely go into another place," artist Keith Haring said, "you're tapping into things that are totally universal, completely beyond your ego and your own self. That's what it's all about."

Must is both the journey and the destination, the upward journey of our lives that guides us toward that higher place, the oneness of all things, the ultimate source of Must.

" ...MUSIC HEARD SO DEEPLY
THAT IT IS NOT HEARD AT ALL, BUT YOU ARE THE MUSIC
WHILE THE MUSIC LASTS. "

T.S. ELIOT
FOUR QUARTETS

THE SOURCE OF
YOUR MUST

↓

THE SOURCE OF
EVERYONE'S MUST

MUST THROUGHOUT TIME

This journey isn't new; it is, perhaps, one of mankind's oldest endeavors. In some Inuit and Native American tribes, members would embark on vision quests to gain personal enlightenment. They would go into the wild for days, often fasting. The journey's purpose was to reconnect with nature and the spiritual realm, and through this immersion, have dreams or waking visions to give them guidance. Australian aborigines would go on walkabouts, journeys taken as an entry into adulthood, sometimes lasting several months.

When Nipun Mehta was at the peak of building his company ServiceSpace, he felt a deep calling to go to India. He ended up selling his company and convincing his new wife to join him on a pilgrimage. They flew to India and for three months they walked. Later, he asked the graduating class of the University of Pennsylvania, "Have you ever thought of something and then just known it had to happen? This was one of those things." Together, they encountered the generosity of complete strangers, marveled at the natural world, and most of all, learned about themselves. "Don't just go through life," he urged, ". . . make it a point, instead, to acknowledge mystery and welcome rich questions—questions that nudge you towards a greater understanding of this world and your place in it."

Over time, you will reach a point on your journey when you are so far down your path that suddenly, you will look around to see that you have created a world and this world has created you—step by step, line by line, your dream in real life.

"I DREAM MY PAINTING AND THEN I PAINT MY DREAM."

VINCENT VAN GOGH

MUST OVER A LIFETIME

Mary Ellen Geist's father played in a band on nights and weekends throughout his life. In a letter to physician and author Oliver Sacks, she wrote of her father, who continued to play his music even while suffering from Alzheimer's for thirteen years.

> *The plaque has apparently invaded a large amount of his brain.... He has no idea what he did for a living, where he is living now, or what he did ten minutes ago. Almost every memory is gone. Except for the music. In fact, he opened for the Radio City Music Hall Rockettes in Detroit this past November.... The evening he performed, he had no idea how to tie a tie ... he got lost on the way to the stage—but the performance? Perfect.*

We each have unique potential that was given to us at birth, but whether or not we cultivate it is entirely up to us. In its purest sense, Must is why we are here to begin with, and choosing it is the journey of our lives.

IF YOU BELIEVE TH

SPECIAL INSIDE OF YOU, A

YOU GAVE IT A SHOT, HONO

SMALL WAY — TODAY.

STOMACH BECAUSE YOU CAN SEE

YOUR DREAMS AND YOUR DA

TIGHTEN YOUR GRIP ON W

IF YOU'VE BEEN PEERIN

MUST BUT CAN'T G

DIG A LITTLE DEEPER AN

STOPPING YOU — TO

IS A RECURRIN

AND IT OCCURS AT

OF TWO ROADS. WE ARRIVE

YOU HAVE SOMETHING
YOU FEEL IT'S ABOUT TIME
HAT CALLING IN SOME
YOU FEEL A KNOT IN YOUR
ENORMOUS DISTANCE BETWEEN
REALITY, DO ONE THING TO
T YOU WANT — TODAY.
OWN THE ROAD TO
E MAKE THE CHOICE,
IND OUT WHAT'S
AY. BECAUSE THERE
CHOICE IN LIFE,
THE INTERSECTION
IS PLACE AGAIN AND AGAIN.

And *today*, you get to choose.

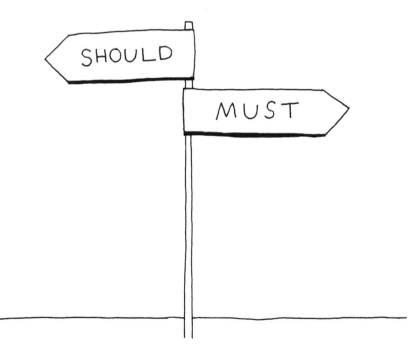

Hungarian pianist András Schiff concluded his performance of Bach's French Suites to thunderous applause at the San Francisco Symphony. The man next to me clapped loudly.

I leaned over and asked, "What did you think?"

"Tremendous, absolutely tremendous," he said. "You know, I've downloaded his performances and listened to his records for years, but this—to be here in the third row where the strings vibrate in your chest, where his hands flutter over the keys as he plays for three hours . . . from memory . . . with his eyes closed—*this* is to see something with soul in it."

"Wow," I said, "you must be a pianist."

"Who, me?" he said. "No, I can't play a tune. But I often have a dream where I can."

ABOUT THE AUTHOR

Elle Luna paints, designs, and writes. She also runs a textile venture, the Bulan Project, a collaboration between designers and master batik artists in Bali, and has previously worked as a designer at IDEO and with startups including Mailbox, Medium, and Uber. She speaks to groups around the world, sharing the story of "The Crossroads of Should and Must," and lives in San Francisco and online at *elleluna.com*.

SPECIAL THANKS TO

MY PUBLISHING FAMILY

TED WEINSTEIN ♥ BRUCE TRACY ♥ SUZIE BOLOTIN
PAGE EDMUNDS ♥ JAMES WEHRLE ♥ STEVEN PACE ♥ SELINA MEERE
JESSICA WIENER ♥ BETH LEVY ♥ CLAIRE MCKEAN
BECKY TERHUNE ♥ DOUG WOLFF ♥ VAUGHN ANDREWS
MARILYN BARNETT ♥ ADELIA KALYVAS ♥ JOHN JENKINSON
WALTER WEINTZ ♥ DAVID SCHILLER

MY FAMILY FAMILY FAMILY

ELLIE &
JIM BEATON

MARY D. &
EARL LUNA

MARY &
ROBERT E.
LUNA

ELE &
HUNTLEY
LUNA

TILLY
THE SWEETEST
DOGGIE IN
ALL THE
LANDS

MY
GRANDPARENTS

M♥M & DAD

BROTHER &
SISTER-IN-LAW

& ♥ MY FUTURE NIECE? NEPHEW?
WHO WE CANNOT WAIT TO MEET !!!!!!!!

MY ASTRAL PLANE FAMILY

● ☾ ☾ ☽ ◯ ◯ ◯ ◯ ◯ ◗ ◗ ◗ ◗ ●

EMILY LAFAVE ♥ GENTRY UNDERWOOD ♥ MICHAEL GALPERT
KRISTINA ENSMINGER ♥ CAMILLE RICKETS ♥ CRAIG MOD ♥ KATE LEE
SARA FRISK ♥ LIGAYA TICHY ♥ NICOLE SCHUETZ ♥ DARYA ROSE ♥
♥ MICHELLE UNDERWOOD ♥ RONAN UNDERWOOD ♥ AUSTIN UNDERWOOD
AMBER RAE ♥ FARHAD ATTAIE ♥ SHARON BURKA ♥ ROB LAFAVE ♥
♥ APRIL WATERS ♥ DAVID NOËL ♥ ANNESSA BRAYMER ♥ SARAH OWEN ♥
SANDY SPEICHER ♥ SARA WILLIAMS ♥ EVAN WILLIAMS ♥ OM MALIK
MICHAEL O'NEAL ♥ ZOFI TINKOFF ♥ SUNNY BATES ♥ NINA PACKER
ALEJANDRA CISNEROS ♥ ANAK AGUNG SRI ARINI ♥ I NYOMAN NONDERAN
♥ NI WAYAN PELUNG ♥ NI MADE RENI ♥ NI MADE KARIASTI ♥
NI WAYAN SUGI MULIYANI ♥ THE LAHEYS ♥ THE VASCONCELOSES,
AND AN ANGEL FROM BEYOND, SUSIE HERRICK ♥

I'VE BEEN INFLUENCED AND INSPIRED IN
WRITING THIS BOOK BY THE ARTIST'S WAY
BY JULIA CAMERON, SIDDHARTHA BY HERMANN HESSE,
THE ENNEAGRAM IN LOVE & WORK BY HELEN PALMER,
THE POWER OF MYTH BY JOSEPH CAMPBELL, AND THE
WORK OF DR. CLARISSA PINKOLA ESTÉS.

A
SPECIAL
SUPER
FABULOUS
MAGICAL AMAZING
OUT-OF-THIS-WORLD

THANK YOU
TO MY EDITOR
MARY ELLEN O'NEILL

WHOSE BEAUTIFUL, GENEROUS
SPIRIT SHAPED AND ENLIGHTENED
EVERY PAGE OF THIS BOOK.

CREDITS

For a list of the quotations cited and the sources used in writing this book, please go to *choosemust.com*.

The photograph on pages 12 and 13 is by San Francisco–based photographer Loren Baxter. The portrait on page 157 is by New York–based photographer Ike Edeani.

The book is set in FF Tisa, a typeface designed by Mitja Miklavčič in 2008 and the original typeface in which "The Crossroads of Should and Must" first appeared on *Medium.com* on April 8, 2014.

The book was written in Ubud, Bali, during the rice harvest while sitting at a wooden table in The House Without Walls; written in the magical, wondrous cottage from my childhood in Grand Haven, Michigan; written in autumn in New York at the Ace Hotel, sprawled across room 1007; and it was completed where it began, in San Francisco, California, in the white room from my dreams.

SHARE YOUR THOUGHTS
#CHOOSEMUST